DRESS TO DIGITALLY IMPRESS

Techniques for Succesful Video Interviews

Karen Mathis

CONTENTS

Title Page	
DRESS TO DIGITALLY IMPRESS	1
Introduction	3
I. Communicate a Positive First Impression on Camera	10
II. Express Your Best Identity	16
III. Consider Psychology of Dress	22
IV. Use Meanings of Color to Communicate	24
V. Choose Silhouettes for Cultural Power	34
VI. How to Receive the Best Attributions	39
VII. Video tips and links	41
References	47
Acknowledgement	49
About The Author	51
Books By This Author	53

DRESS TO DIGITALLY IMPRESS

Techniques for Successful Video Interviews

The Classic Blue Jacket - Expresses authority, intelligence, and high-standards for men and women~ Karen Mathis

Soft tailoring and pinstripes are a winning combination. This outfit expresses authority, positive energy, sophistication, intelligence, and high capabilities ~ Karen Mathis

INTRODUCTION

Unprecedented is the word used most to describe life as we know it... at least for now in 2020. Trends and markets are changes that challenge the way of life and work. While some companies have furloughed employees and put a freeze on hiring new ones, others are exploring ways to keep business going by recruiting new employees. The big global companies like Google, Amazon and Facebook have announced their move to online job interviews for the duration of the Coronavirus outbreak. Global recruiters are joining in pushing video conferencing apps. Zoom and WeChat Work are a couple apps that are up in growth nearly fivefold since January 2020. Virtual interviews may replace in-person ones for a while, and maybe forever.

In researching for this book, I learned that even before the pandemic companies were moving to remote jobs in great numbers. My hope is that you will better understand the **what, why, and how** of video interviews to increase your chances for success. Whether it's getting a job during and after the COVID-19 pandemic or pursuing freedom from spending years of your life working in an office. The list of possible remote jobs and links to new articles and surveys can be found in Chapter VII of the book. It certainly makes the case that remote jobs are seriously legit.

Just imagine being able to choose your own work environment. Perhaps you like to travel, after the limits of this pandemic are lifted, you might be able to be in a different country each month and maintain full-time employment with a remote job. This is already the case for many knowledge-based workers. Whether performing job interviews or another form of online presentation, there's new valuable information you need to know to put new choices in your hands. Mastering your video job interview might even lead to a new life-changing journey.

Remote Jobs Stats

I was surprised to learn just how far the workplace had moved to remote jobs even before this pandemic
(Flexjobs.com 2019 Annual Survey):

- 76% of professionals prefer fully remote work options.
- 74% of respondents believe that flexible working has become the "new normal."
- Having a choice of working from home is now a key factor for those evaluating new career opportunities.
- 65% of respondents think they are more productive working from their home office.

Over the last five years remote work grew by 44%. FlexJobs.com and Global Workplace Analytics found that between 2005 to 2017, there was a 159% increase in remote work. In 2015, 3.9 million U.S. workers were working remotely. Today that number is at 4.7 million, or 3.4% of the population (Retrieved from Flexjobs.com). Just imagine how that will probably increase with the current shelter-in-place process. The influence of the pandemic has the attention of companies and how critical it is to offer it where possible.

Good to know... Research shows companies are using workplace flexibility to attract and retain talent. Certainly, **appearance** will **play a huge role** in getting hired whether in person or **video interviews**. If it's webinars or Zoom meetings with your teams, the same applies.

Prepare and Produce

Although prep for the video job interview will be basically the same as in-person, there's another side to the process. You need to put on your **producer hat**. It's pretty simple, the production required for effective video interviews utilizes a couple new tools worth acquiring.

Those who are already conducting video interviews, have insights to help. Some of the criticism is overall amazement that the candidates haven't managed the basics of image and sound quality. We see this on cable news networks with stay-at-home announcers interviewing stay-at-home guests from their homes. Sometimes we can hear but the sometimes-scary pixelated images on the screen completely distract from their messages. As HR and managers conduct video job interviews, they want to see and hear from their candidates. FYI some of their comments and complaints include: poor camera views, connectivity issues, poor sound quality, distracting backgrounds, and distracting locations.

Although this book's main focus is your first impression appearance, and we will get to that... I wanted to first address a few of these production issues that are tripping up applicants and presenters. If you look good but your words cannot be heard, that's a problem. What this means is Appearance for video interviews just expanded. When planning for your video presentations, include backgrounds, surroundings, sounds, connectivity, and whatever else could become a distraction.

As for your personal image at your presentation, there is key information here to help you plan. Also the new book, Power of Appearance, is loaded with research of over 40 social psych studies, as well as stylist tools for getting your best image expressed. The first part of the book is a parable, so the reader can experience a step-by-step process of empowering appearance along with the main character, who is getting ready for a major job interview.

Silk scarf at the neck expresses high standards and sophistication. It frames the face bringing all attention to you and your presentation. For video it is best in solids of understated geometrics in colors that enhance your natural coloring ~ Karen Mathis

What to Wear

As long as humans are dealing with humans, appearance will continue to be primary in helping to win over an audience. Planning what to wear for your webinar, video interview or presentation begins with your goals. Once you know what choices are most important, you can evaluate how to connect best with your audience. This is the basis of choosing what to wear.

How do you empower your appearance? The following is a summary of key information. Your choices within each of these will determine success:

1. Important to wear colors that enhance your personal best features.
2. How to use fit in your favor.

3.   Accessorize to communicate positive cultural nonverbal messages.

4.   Use fabrics such as silk to communicate higher standards.

5.   Understand a few basics of the psychology of how to dress for best results.

Why does appearance matter so much?

So, life has changed. What's the one important thing at an interview that hasn't changed? It's your *first impression*. In a Nanosecond, an impression of you is formed based solely on appearance. That's why your clothing choices can make all the difference in how you impress on your video presentation. It's how you communicate your personal identity to others before you speak a word on camera.

Your **first impression** will be established at the very first moment your video becomes live. Everything on camera is a little more exaggerated. Facial expressions, voice, colors, visuals all become just a little more on camera.

Are you smiling? If so, it will be read as a positive and make you look self-confident. If you have even the slightest serious expression it might be read of insecure, fearful, not confident for the job, not a nice person, and maybe even not someone who can be trusted.

Have you groomed the best hairstyle to frame your face? Messy hair or extreme hair styles can grab all the attention. When your face is covered with hair, you cannot make eye contact where trust and so much more is established.

Is your make-up application balanced? Again, be sure your make-up is only a supporting role and not competing by being too stark or strong. In general stay away from extremes. Any make-up added should help you appear healthy. Even guys may need a little powder to get rid of a shiny nose and forehead. The interviewer's focus needs to be on your words and attitude, and not distracted by a shiny forehead. This is why tv announcers and sports announcers use a touch of powder.

Are you dressed in your best confidence-building outfit? Assignments will be made based on what's seen and believed about you in that first Nano-flash. You get one chance… and it will be lasting. Choose items that help you express your personal best without stealing the show. Chapters I through VI contribute more information to help you choose wisely.

A few studies on the psychology of dress are present to answer why we make the effort in clothing choices. The purpose is to guide you for best results with your particular audience. This is a subject that isn't taught in school. Most people learn what they can from their parents, friends, and role models. Think through who influenced you the most and who you would like to look like. You may find actors from the movies, fashion magazines, and the music industry are standouts. These guides tend to be extreme but can work as long as they serve you. Consider your clothing as a second skin on the body. It expresses our personal identity to others.

Nonverbal Communication

Since facial expression, grooming, and clothing makes up what goes into a first impressions, clothing is primary in expressing your image. For that reason, we do a deeper dive and look at what clothing choices might mean to you. For example, your clothing is considered to be *nonverbal communication.* Deconstruct what you want expressed regarding who you are to others. The information in POWER of Appearance along with additional downloads at the Power of Appearance website, provide tools to create the message you want communicated.

Psychology of Clothing

In the study, Dress, Body and Self: Research in the Social and Psychology of Dress done by Kim Johnson, Sharron J Lennon & Nancy Rudd we learn that what we wear influences others in their reactions. This can weigh heavily when choosing an outfit for your presentation. The study is focused on two broad areas: (1) dress as a stimulus and its influence on (a) attributions by others, attributions about self, and on one's behavior and (2) relationships between dress, the body, and the self.

"The social psychology of dress is concerned with how an individual's dress affects the behavior of self as well as the behavior of others toward the self," (Johnson & Lennon 2014).

There's so much more to clothing than meets the eye. Fashion is your greatest tool of personal expression. Without going too deep, this book touches on the psychology of clothing.

❖ ❖ ❖

I. COMMUNICATE A POSITIVE FIRST IMPRESSION ON CAMERA

A. *First Impression Facts*

It's fascinating how in a nanosecond our brains establish beliefs about one another. How does this happen without knowing anything about the person? It's called *nonverbal communication*. Other than facial expression and grooming, our clothing "tells all" about who you are to others. The power of appearance has been confirmed in years of research.

Let's focus on your plan for a successful first impression at your future virtual presentation. The goal is to create an appearance that earns respect.

Why Does It Matter? Check out the following reasons it matters what you wear:

- It signals social status

- It defines roles
- It points out authority
- It teaches timely appropriateness
- Historically, it establishes cultural value including differentiation

> Clothing is part of a larger context of your appearance, even when you don't think that much about what you are wearing.
>
> www.POWERofAppearance.com

B. Clothing

Clothing, and fashion have a strong connection to communication. It has been a subject for psychological research dating back to William James (1890/1983). In fact, clothing is such an effective nonverbal communication tool it can even help build your self-esteem. When you get it wrong, it can send you down a path that leads to being disrespected or overlooked.

The clothing you choose has meaning way beyond comfort and body coverage. The visual communication it sends out on your behalf empowers your appearance in ways words cannot express as effectively.

J. S. Bowman in his 1992 study surveyed personnel officials from four different agencies: departments of administration, finance, and commerce and the executive office of the governor in all 50 states.

They found that **75% of the managers** believed **employees who were well-dressed** and groomed were **perceived to be more intelligent, hardworking, and socially acceptable** than those dressed casually. **Respondents** who dressed more formally established a **higher level of respect and authority** necessary to get their jobs done. In this study it is important to note that **casually dressed employees did not command** or show respect based on their agency norms (Karl et al., 2013).

How can you use this information? **Look into dress codes** whether official or implied for the jobs of interest and/or audience of your presentation. Remember, even if you're interviewing for a job in an industry that expects casual dress, a mix of casual and business formal will empower your appearance. For example, for men that could be a polo and blazer, for women that could be either t-shirt and jacket, or a silk blouse and scarf. For creative careers, the guidelines expand, and the options can include more extreme current fashion trends. Certain silhouettes and accessories express just how up to speed you are on fashion without saying a word. It's all about your audience!

On the other hand, casual has its place, too. Studies show we bond on the casual. Use your tees and jeans for Zooming with friends.

The following 5 points will help you express power in your appearance:

1. Again, silk expresses higher standards
2. Gold and precious stones express value worthy of royalty
3. Pearls express honesty, innocence, and sophistication
4. Bespoke expresses wealth and says you are "the boss"
5. Well-fitted tailored jacket expresses authority and intelligence (K.Mathis, 2020).

C. Grooming

Grooming, style, and facial expressions also have impact. All are important non-verbal communication tools. Learning about this subject helps direct better choices. Keep hair out of your eyes, if possible show your eyebrows. They help with positive facial expressions. For long hair, sweep it away from your face. Remember, who is the star of your show? Your hair or you? Keep hair under control and be sure it enhances your face without competing for attention.

D. Facial Expressions

Smiling is always best at an interview, and at a video interview it will require additional smiles. It also takes a lot more energy and expression. Turn everything up a notch. A straight face translates to a bored image. Give them some of your personality to remember you by.

How do you make eye contact with your computer or iPhone screen? There is a camera location. It isn't the screen and it isn't the little feedback image of you. If you look at those two things, you will not be looking into the eyes of the interviewer. Remember, **making eye contact** at a video interview is **looking only at the camera** part of the screen.

Practice making a video. Note: As tempting as it can be, avoid looking at yourself at the small feedback image of you… cover it up if necessary. You need only be concerned with the camera.

E. Body Language

"Physical presence has a major impact on empowering first impressions," (Mathis, 2020). It has the same effect on us that clothing does cognitively. It sends messages to others and beliefs within ourselves. The point is that **you will perform better** if you **activate positive nonverbal body language**. Check out Ted Talks on body language and the benefits the Superman or Superwoman pose just before an interview or presentation. It is empowering and builds confidence. One of my favorites is Amy Cuddy's Ted Talk.

Active Nonverbal Body Language – Use these!
1. Make solid eye contact with a positive expression.
2. Sit tall with straight posture with shoulders back to represent alertness.
3. Hold head high and chest open.
4. Smile to bring in positive energy.
5. Direct eye contact with the camera eye and smile to express confidence.
6. Hands down to your sides out of view unless you need to gesture.

Passive Nonverbal Body Language – Stay away from these!
1. Dropping the head down says = "I am not important."
2. Hunched shoulders = "I should probably just give up trying."

3. Slumping to appear smaller.
4. Crossed and defensive almost holding and comforting oneself says, "I don't belong."
5. Looking down or bashful – "I'm not worthy" or "I'm afraid and I don't know what I'm doing."

F. Video Production is now part of your first impression.

Background becomes part of what is seen. One of your favorite paintings behind your head may distract the interviewer. While you are sharing your innermost desires for the perfect job or promoting your new book, they may be trying to make out what is in the painting. In a studio there is usually a designed background or solid one. Try to **find a place at home or private office** that is **quiet** and one that doesn't have distractions in the background.

Sound is now part of your first impression. If the interviewer cannot hear you clearly, it will be a negative experience. Find sound options on your computer. For Mac it is in System Preferences. If you have a microphone, set it up and use it. If you can only use earbuds, keep in mind that they can be distracting so camo them if possible. Be sure to do a sound check with a friend ahead of your interview either way.

◆ ◆ ◆

II. EXPRESS YOUR BEST IDENTITY

Navy or Black blazer and blue pinstripe shirts have been established as formal business attire going back to the 1900's. Pinstripes were established by the banking industry. This combinination for men or women is a statment of power, authority, and intelligence ~ Karen Mathis

A. Who are you again?

Who are you, and what are your **specific goals?** The answers to these questions **are central** to choosing what to wear for your interview or anytime. Take time to dream! I like to reverse engineer life when planning goals. Where do you want to be in 10 years? It may even be a question at your interview. What do you want to be doing at that time? What accomplishments would you like to have acquired? How much money will you make? What else in your life will be a priority? These questions will assist you in realizing that you have choices! How can your presentation align with helping you reach what's most important to you?

Next **explore what jobs or opportunities will help et you there**. Connect the dots... and put your best plan together for reaching your ultimate goals.

Next **deconstruct each item on your list** into parts. **Reconstruct a plan of action** to be sure it can be accomplished. What's missing? Perhaps an online class or certification is required. Explore it and you may be surprised at what you find. There are many free online classes at the moment due to the pandemic.

Expand your options and **find your next steps**. This is meditative work that is done best when you include what is meaningful. Putting energy into work that is **meaningful and aligned with your goals** is one of the key principles to self-motivation. A book worth reading on this subject is *Master Your Motivation* written by Susan Fowler. I had the good fortune of being a student in one of her classes in my master's program. It was there that I perfected my own personal mission. This book can be a completely new approach to finding self-motivation. I had many aha moments while reading the book!

B. The Appearance Plan

There are two additional important reasons you want to look your personal best:

1. Outwardly you will be **empowered with positive** assumptions from others called "**assignments**." For example, they may believe you are, "a smart person," "a nice person," and "would fit in well with us."

"The inferences we make about another person's character and status are made from how we perceive her or his appearance," (P. A. Andersen, 1984).

2. Inwardly there's a cognitive reaction to looking your best, called *Enclothed Cognition*. It's the very reason some of the British private schools have students wearing their blazers on test days. They simply perform better. Research shows what works for students is the same for working adults. **Increased self-confidence results in improved performance**.

First step is to **consider your audience**. It's worth finding out whether there's a spoken or unspoken dress code at play. Google the name of the company + executives. You may find a company list with pictures. Most will be dressed in a mix of business formal. For men that can be shirt and jacket without a tie. For women it can be turtleneck or blouse with a vest or jacket. This can be a guide as to how formal or casual their leaders dress.

Next **plan how** you need to look to **fit in with the tribe**. Remember, how you dress is not a frivolous exercise. It's a **form of communication**. *Nonverbal* is one more way to speak another's language. Whether you realize it or not, your appearance will be screaming your identity, non-verbally. Let's get you in total control of that messaging.

In order to accomplish our task, the following key filters need to be established for you, personally:

1. YOUR PERSONAL COLOR PALETTE: Wear a color that is in harmony with your natural coloring. You may download the free Do-it-yourself Color evaluation tool at PowerofAppearance.com. It will help you quickly establish your best harmony and contrast colors.

Did you know **color is used** as a tool **in the memory process**? Our brains actually use it like a camera that takes a color photo but it's a memory. Colors also have cultural meanings that create emotional reactions, as well. This is one of the reasons big marketing companies to to such trouble choosing colors for ads, book covers, and more. Color matters. You can use it to your benefit, as well.

It's important to note that black and neutrals don't necessarily trigger memory. Mainly they don't give the brain anything to hold onto. The positive is that you can wear a good black suit over and over with different accessories without it being noticed. Helpful info when working on a limited budget.

Black is great to wear as long as you accessorize with color. Black can be dramatic and provide great contrast to color. However, black or other neutrals are not good without an effective use of color preferably near your face. All black will not give the brain anything to hook onto to remember you. **Wearing a solid silk scarf** in one of your **personal harmony or contrasting colors** will solve the challenge and make sure you are memorable. You can find out the difference of harmony and contrasting colors if you evaluate your personal colors. Consider using it for free Do-it-yourself Color evaluation tool.

2. SHAPE, FIT, AND BEST SILHOUETTES: Have you heard of the **Authority Principle**? More about this is spelled out in the POWER of Appearance book and it works in your favor when wearing a tailored blazer or jacket. Respect is immediately assigned to you based on silhouette and the fit.

In the POWER of Appearance book, the main character learns where to hem and alter her garments based on another stylist tool called the Indent's Tool. At your virtual interview since no one can see your back, you can make temporary changes for effect. You can always get them permanently tailored after you get the job.

Just as magazine photo shoots may have clothespins or safety pins out of sight of the camera, you can do that, too. Pinning in a jacket from inside helps create an indent at your natural waist for a better look. Research shows that perfect fit empowers appearance. Think James Bond in his Bespoke suits.

3. FABRICS THAT REPRESENT QUALITY: Silk sets higher quality standards based on its long cultural and historic use. Adding a strip of silk at the neck will send a message of sophistication and accomplishment. Using tropical weight wools, linens and other fine fabrics will be worth the effort.

4. FRAME THE FACE: Often I ask my clients, **"Who's the star of your show?"** In other words, not the shoes, not the hair, not the bag. When evaluating an outfit, everything should always support your face. For your virtual interview it should definitely be your face. Just like any painting on your walls, add a frame and it rises in stature. **Use your hair, make-up, and accessories as tools** to frame your face. Think of them as supporting characters. This way all eyes are on you and your presentation.

When **adding scarves** use your personal contrast colors for the most dramatic and memorable effect. Please stay away from busy prints. Sweeping or setting hair back away from your eyes is best. Showing your eyebrows for expression will enhance your looks.

Note: Research tells us to beware that showing too much cleavage can cost promotions based on the decision makers.

Add quality jewelry if you have it to establish power. Both gold and silver hold cultural power that will translate to your appearance.

If you apply these tips, at your interview, YOU will be the star of the show!

The 3 piece suit is a statement of ultimate authority. It is considered business formal. The white shirt and tie add sophistication.

III. CONSIDER PSYCHOLOGY OF DRESS

A. *Employ the Authority Principle*

It was Bickman (1974), who pointed out that **formal dress increases perceptions of dominance** and control. Joseph & Alex, (1972) showed the correlation between **specific silhouettes and attire** to establish **positions of authority**, called the *Authority Principle.*

When you wear certain silhouettes and accessories, there is a history in our culture that assigns meaning to those silhouettes and naturally attributes certain characteristics to the wearer. Use this information wisely when dressing for certain professions that require confidence and authority. **Wear a suit jacket or sports jacket, and tie when you need the influence**.

B. *Employ Enclothed Cognition*

> In a study by Adam Galinsky and Hajo Adam, they proposed that clothing "involves the co-occurrence of two independent factors – the symbolic meaning of the clothes and the physical experience of wearing them," (2012). They coined

the term *enclothed cognition* to describe t**he systematic influence clothes have on the wearer's psychological processes.** It is why a lab coat experiment with random college students showed they performed best cognitively when they believed the lab coat was a doctor's lab coat versus the ones that believed they were wearing a painter's jacket. This and other studies are outlined in Power of Appearance.

IV. USE MEANINGS OF COLOR TO COMMUNICATE

Use solid colors for your video interview. The star of the show is YOU... not a printed top or tie. Choose colors that enhance your natural coloring. If you have a light complexion then choose medium to dark colors next to your face for contrast. If you have a darker complexion choose medium and lighter colors next to your face.

Research shows why color matters to your appearance. It has been confirmed that color plays a pivotal role in all our visual experiences.

Color Importance to First Impressions:
Research revealed that within 90 seconds of initial viewing a person, people make a subconscious judgment about them, the environment, or product, and that between 62% and 90% of that assessment is based on color alone. *(CCICOLOR - Institute for Color Research).*

There is Power in Color
- 92% Believe color presents an image of impressive qual-

ity

- 90% Feel color can assist in attracting new customers

- 90% Believe customers remember presentations and documents better when color is used
- 83% Believe color makes them appear more successful

- 81% Think color gives them a competitive edge

- 76% Believe that the use of color makes their business appear larger to clients (*colorcom.com/research/why-color-matters*).

Color can aid in helping you to be remembered by others. Since color is used as a tool to aid memory, choosing the right colors to wear is important. Download my free Color Evaluation Stylist Tool.

Color Evaluation

- Using a mirror and natural light look closely at your hair, eyes, and skin to find which color on the color wheel above best represents each one of them.
- Look closely to find the dominant colors and mark the wheel with an "M" for main. Mark each one for hair, eyes, and skin.
- Next look closely at the accent shades in each of the three and mark them with an "A." These are your personal harmony colors.
- Last step go diagonally across each marking of M and A on the color wheel. This time mark the diagonal colors with a C for Contrast. (should have 6 C's. These are your colors that help you stand out!

You now have your personal color palette to reference when shopping or choosing what to wear for best results..

www.POWERofAppearance.com

The following are cultural meanings to a few colors:

A. Red – Communicates Power in our Culture and Here's Why:

  ~The Power of Fire & Blood
  ~Red Letter Word of Christ
  ~Red Sky
  ~Red Flags of Communism, Christian, and Islamic, Redline ~Between Church and State, Dante's Inferno.
  ~The Love and Fashion of Roses
  ~Red Hearts & Valentine's Day
  ~Lady in Red
  ~Red Heads
  ~Chanel Red, Dior Red, and MORE!

B. Blue = Communicates Power of Intelligence & Creativity!

~Blue as the color of the sky and ocean represents calmness and coolness of water.
~It's associated with creativity and intelligence.
~It symbolizes loyalty, strength, wisdom, and trust.
~Blue is sincere, reserved and quiet.
~It's reliable and responsible and radiates security and trust.
~Blue Lowers Metabolism (Jacob Olesen).

C. Black – Communicates Power of Sophistication and Mystery!

~The Color Black relates to the hidden, secretive, and the unknown.
~Black is associated with power, fear, mystery, strength, authority, elegance, formality, death, evil, and aggression.
~It is prestigious.
~Black is the absorption of all color and the absence of light.
~Black hides, while white brings to light.

D. Yellow – Communicates Value and Beauty!

~ Yellow Represents Freshness
~ It can mean Sunshine and Happiness.
~ Also, sun reference equals Energy.
~ It is positivity and Clarity.
~ Sunny outlook of Optimism.
~ Enlightenment, Remembrance, Intellect, and Honor.
~ The color of Loyalty and Joy.

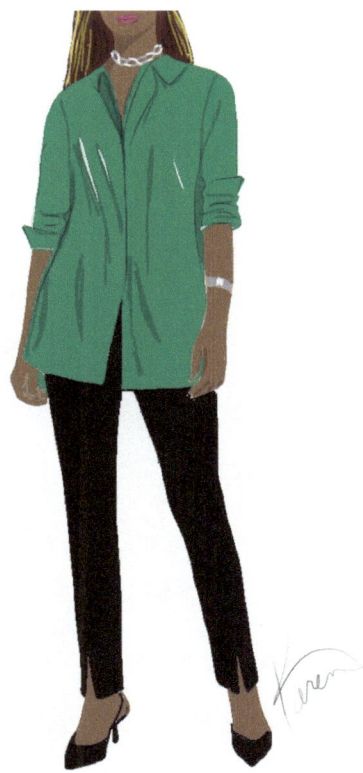

E. Green – Communicates Healing Power and Wealth!

~Color of Life Renewal, Nature, and Energy.
~Associated with Meanings of Growth, Harmony, Freshness, Safety, Fertility, and Environment.
~Traditionally Associated with Money, Finances, Banking, Ambition, Greed, Jealousy, and Wall Street.
~Visible to the Human Eye and the Dominant Color in Nature.
~Common in the Spring Season when all of the plants are coming back to life.
~Helps alleviate anxiety, depression, and nervousness.
~Also brings with it a sense of hope, health, adventure, and renewal.
~Self-control, compassion, and harmony.

~Green is often used to indicate safety (BourneCreative.com).

F. Purple – Communicates Supernatural POWER!

~Purple since rarely seen in nature, gives it a supernatural image.
~Purple is the most powerful visible wavelength of electromagnetic energy. "Only a few steps away from X-rays and Gamma," (Colormatters.com).
~It is associated with Supernatural and the Cosmos.
~It symbolizes "magic, mystery, spirituality, the subconscious, creativity, dignity, royalty, and it evokes all of these

meanings more than any other colors," (Colormatters.com)

V. CHOOSE SILHOUETTES FOR CULTURAL POWER

A. Jackets - Tailored jackets communicate authority, strength, wealth, and intelligence.

Blazers are usually solid colors mostly navy or black but occassionally bright colors work for social events. Also, white and patterns come out in the Springtime for sporting events like The Kentucky Derby. Historically blue and white stripes are introduced in fashion as part of a nautical theme. Blazers can be single or double breasted. Most classics have naval inspired metal buttons. They're suitable for both men and women. They are usually more business formal than a sports coat, and less formal than a tailored suit. Designers show them in a variety of fabrics such as wool gabardines, flannels, linens, and other wool blends. They work well with a variety of slacks for men such as khakis, tropical weight wools, gabardines in neutrals. Blazers can be worn with shirts and ties, t-shirts, cashmere sweaters, polo knit shirts for women and men.

History of the Blazer

The sartorial blazer became known for its exclusivity throughout history. In 1748 the double-breasted navy blazer with brass buttons became the uniform of the Royal Navy. In 1825 bright red blazers were the dress of St John's College Boat Club in Cambridge. Blazers signify victory in two sports, the Congressional Cup Regatta at Long Beach Yacht Club and the Masters golf tournament, held in Augusta, Georgia. In the 1960's and early 1970's during the British Music Invasion where Beatles and other bands such as The Rolling Stones, The Kinks, The Yardbirds and others wore striped blazers/boating jackets, and brightly colored blazers. They became a staple for career women by 2000. Women added styling such as rolled up sleeves, various lapel sizes and shapes, and added new colors and trims.

B. Tailored Suit – *It is the ultimate business-formal attire that expresses the total authority, confidence, and control.* It's difficult to look at the history of the men's suit without acknowledging the traditional *Saville Row Suit.* It is the traditional bespoke process done by tailors of Saville Row, a street in London's Mayfair district, since the late 18th century. Early in the 19th century tailors began adjusting styles inspired by English horseback riding clothes. Tailors created suits to epitomize modern male fashion. It was so successful that it dominated for more than a century. The rigorous attention to fit that might require up to 25 or more fittings. Today the same processes and in some cases sewing machines are still in use on Saville Row. The process begins with the cutter, who takes the fittings with the clients, cuts the jacket, and oversees the entire process. Each tailor has a specialty for example the finisher puts on the buttonholes. There's a tailor for creating the lapel, one for putting in the zipper in the pants, making the pants, cutting and applying the lining, sewing in the sleeves and the pockets. It involves a house of tailors that touch each suit.

Firsts:

~Ozwald Boateng, the first black tailor to open on Savile Row, launched the first Headquarters in May 2002. He is known for rich patterned textiles, an influence from his native Ghana. He introduced his first womenswear collection May 6, 2019 at the tents in Bryant Park. Retrieved from https://ozwaldboateng.co.uk/history

~Kathryn Sargent has become the first female master tailor to open her shop on London's historic Savile Row. "As a tailor it has been a long-held ambition of mine. I am thrilled to be making history, although for me being a woman is incidental - I am a tailor first and foremost,"(bbc.com/news/uk-england-london-35977446) Sargent completed her fashion design degree and began an apprenticeship at Gieves & Hawkes. In 2009 she became head cutter as the first woman in Savile Row history to hold that position. In the interview she mentioned that just 20 years ago to have a women in the cutting room was very unusual. She says she has been very welcomed. Retrieved from https://www.bbc.com/news/uk-england-london-35977446

~Phoebe Gormley became the first Savile Row tailor through her business name of Gormley and Gamble to cater solely to women. Although she had a rocky start, dropping out of school and launching her company at age 20, she finally made it to Savile Row, a big change from the City-based bicycle shed turned into fitting room. Once she was offered a concession by James Sleater, co-founder of Cad & The Dandy. The new location gave her the deserved credibility of being a real tailor on Savile Row. In 2016 she launched her online business and later a non-profit organization to support other female entrepreneurs. "If I knew what I know now, I don't think I would have been brave enough to do it," Ms. Gormley says. Retrieved from https://www.ft.com/content/7083482e-ac7b-11e9-8030-530adfa879c2

~In **1974 Giorgio Armani** opened his own label and launched his first collection. Inspired by mid-century Italian cinema, he designed finely tailored suits in lighter weight fabrics without the stiffness of the interlinings. His goal was to soften the suit and make it more like a second skin for the wearer. His redefined suits were meant for both women and men. His look redefined business attire and dominated fashion in the 1970s and 1980s. The 2020 Prive' Armani runway show.

~While the wider shoulders and pant legs were the style in 1991, **Carlo Brandelli** designed narrow trousers, and slim modern silhouettes beginning in 1992 with his Squire Gallery. It was a fashion shop that combined art, design and fashion. He later joined Savile Row's Kilgour, a house established in 1880. He is credited for merging his sleek cut Squire suits with the Savile Row's perfection tailoring. His suit evolved to being "Unstructured" without any lining and revealing its total construction. More of his art, design, and fashion can be found on his website.

KAREN MATHIS

VI. HOW TO RECEIVE THE BEST ATTRIBUTIONS

You can evaluate ways to enhance your chances for getting a job during coronavirus and after, using the power of appearance stylist tools. For more information on how to create your best job interview outfit visit www.powerofappearance.com.

> **A. The Perfect Fit** – Tailor a jacket to your body's natural indents. See Indents Tool at www.PowerofAppearance.com
>
> **B. Accessorize for Power**

Use collars, lapels, scarves, ties to frame your face. All accessories are supporting characters for your face. Jewelry can be an effective accessory. Pearls have a cultural meaning of elegance. Silver and Gold jewelry originated with Kings and Queens and has a positive cultural meaning of quality. Accessories express sophistication and elegance.

Accessorizing a plain collar is an opportunity to express quality standards that can bring positive attributes! It's always better to wear solids and add accessories to express rather than flood your appearance with a print that will distract and work against you.

VII. VIDEO TIPS AND LINKS

A. Best Lighting

Lighting is critical to what is seen of you. Lighting should be **in front of you**. If you have a window with a desk in front or table, that can work well for a daytime interview. If the day is cloudy, you will need to bring light in front of your face beside the camera out of view of the camera. It might require two lamps on either side of the laptop adding light to your face. Bright lights behind you will not work. Test a selfie video to see if the lighting is set for the best possible view of your face.

If you are doing a lot of interviewing or planning on frequent Zoom meetings, you may want to invest in a ring light. I found this one in a Google search that includes the tripod as well: https://www.amazon.com/UBeesize-Ringlight-YouTube-Photography-Compatible/dp/B07GDC39Y2/ref=sr_1_3?dchild=1&keywords=ring+light&qid=1587962932&sr=8-3

B. Best Location - Home office or other office – final answer!

C. Internet Connection

Most important is a **solid internet connection.** Wireless might be fine if you must, but you may want to look into direct wired connections to your internet. Old school ethernet wired connection is still best. You'll avoid bad connections and crazy pixilated images of your face which can happen with wireless connection.

D. Camera

#1 choice is to use your laptop or desktop which should have a built-in camera in the screen. If those are not an option, some tablets or smartphones have built-in cameras that might work.

When using a phone or smaller tablet, do not hold it in your hand. Instead buy a selfie tripod stick. They are relatively inexpensive and handy to use.

Be sure to stack books or a box to get the camera at eye level. Selfie tripods come in different heights and might be able to accommodate with their stands. I have two of them, one was about $5 and is only 7" tall but works well on a stack of books to get to eye level. The other is 24" tall and adjusts as needed on a desktop. Old camera stands work, too. They might be able to work from floor up. Whatever it takes **be sure to get the camera at your eye level.**

Avoid looking down at the camera or up to the camera! Stack to eye level.

Wireless remotes: If you haven't used a selfie tripod with your phone, most come with a wireless remote which can be helpful when setting up your iPhone or small tablet. Google

them and find lots of options such as:
Selfie Stick Tripod – Amazon.com https://www.amazon.com/BlitzWolf-Lightweight-Aluminum-Extendable-Bluetooth/dp/B07TG9G8HF?ref_=ast_sto_dp

E. Summary Tips for Success

1. Find a quiet place at home or an office with a door that can close (no public locations).
2. Be sure you have strong internet connectivity. If possible use Ethernet cable.
3. Become familiar with your computer's audio settings. Test microphone.
4. Test your computer's webcam or video if using iPhone.
5. Close apps and sound notifications and place phones and iPad on silent mode.
6. Put pets in a separate room with closed door.
7. Have a copy of your resume, pen and paper.
8. Show you are interested by nodding with a smile when listening.
9. Engage active listening with positive expressions. Smiling sends positive energy!
10. If you wear glasses be sure they are glare proof.

F. Remote Work Resources:

Working from home has become the new norm during this COVID-19 world experiment and will probably be a lasting trend in the workplace. It is attainable for most people as long as you have internet access and a device to connect such as a computer or mobile device.

G. Possible Remote Jobs
1. Software Engineer/Computer & IT/Web developer
2. Audit Manager/Financial Analyst, Controller, Financial Consultant
3. Professional Writer/Editor/Content Creator
4. Video Editor/Animator
5. Supervisory Attorney/Legal
6. Clinical Regulatory Director/Pharmaceutical
7. Environmental Engineer/Natural Sciences Manager/Civil Engineer
8. Quality Improvement/Customer Service Manager
9. Business Development/Marketing Director/Sales Director
10. Academic Professionals/Educational Video Instructor/Curriculum Developer/Master Class
11. Translation Jobs/Copy Editor/Proofreader/Transcriber
12. Research Biologist/Research Scientist/Field Scientist
13. Director of Major Gifts/Principal Gifts Officer/Director of Development/Fundraising Director
14. Professional Business Coach/ Management Consultants
15. Creative Cottage Craft Sewing/Pattern Making/Fashion illustration/Graphic Designer/ Artist
16. Online Entrepreneur/Social Media Brand Ambassador/ Podcasts/ Vlogs/ Unboxings/ eBooks
17. Travel Agents/Customer Service Reps/Corporate Travel Consultants
18. Telephone Nurse/
19. Virtual Assistant/Executive Assistant/Event Planner
20. Outsourced Entrepreneurs/Project Managers
21. Technicians/ support workers in most any field are needed on a part-time or full-time

H. Links to Work-From-Home Career Info

Tips for finding a work-from-home career and ways to avoid scams can be found at: https://www.thebalancecareers.com/work-from-home-careers-3542835

Entrepreneur.com lists 50 opportunities for remote work at: https://www.entrepreneur.com/article/306578

Business Insider published the Highest Paying work-from-home jobs at: https://www.businessinsider.com/highest-paying-work-from-home-jobs-2015-6

Forbes.com blogs ideas for remote jobs and has their list of 27 Best at: https://www.forbes.com/sites/laurabegleybloom/2020/03/31/coronavirus-career-advice-remote-work-from-home-jobs/#431dc8943974

Flexjobs.com explores knowledge workers at: https://www.flexjobs.com/blog/post/knowledge-work-knowledge-worker/

Specific average pay remote jobs are listed at "A Massive List of Work-at-Home Jobs for Reliable Income," at: https://www.theworkathomewoman.com/work-at-home-jobs/

I. Links to Work-From-Home Enhancement

Forbes explores ways to be more effective at your remote work at: https://www.forbes.com/sites/laurabegleybloom/2020/04/13/coronavirus-career-advice-effective-productive-work-from-home/#462499ac27f6

Hope this information will be helpful in your process of video job interviews and digital presentations. Again, most of the personal appearance info applies to in-person interviews, as well. One last tip, usually an in-person interview affords the opportunity to pick up a business card from your interviewer. Since it is so important to follow up, **please remember to get the interviewer's email at the end**.

Enjoy the process and express your best!

REFERENCES

Adam, Hajo, & Galinsky, A.D., (2012). Enclothed Cognition, *Journal of Experimental Social Psychology*, doi:10.1016/j.jesp.2012.02.008

Anderson, Peter A., (2008). *Nonverbal Communication, Forms and Functions*, Second Edition. Waveland Press, Inc., Long Grove, Illinois.

Bickman, L. (1974). The social power of a uniform. *Journal of Applied Social Psychology*, 4(1), 47-61.

Fowler, Susan (2019. Master Your Motivation, Three Scientific Truths for Achieving Your Goals. Berrett-Koehler Publisher, San Francisco, CA,

James, William, (1890). *The Principles of Psychology*. New York: H. Holt and Company.

Johnson, K., Lennon, S.J. & Rudd, N. Dress, body and self: research in the social psychology of dress. *Fashion and Textiles* **1**, 20 (2014). https://doi.org/10.1186/s40691-014-0020-7

Joseph, N., & Alex, N. (1972). The uniform: A sociological perspective, *American Journal of Sociology*, _7_7; 719-730.

Karl, K. A., Hall, L. M., & Peluchette, J. V. (2013). City Employee Perceptions of the Impact of Dress and Appearance: You Are What You Wear. *Public Personnel Management*, *42*(3), 452–470. https://doi.org/10.1177/0091026013495772

Mathis, Karen, (2020). *POWER of Appearance*. Kindle Books sold by Amazon.com.

ACKNOWLEDGEMENT

It is my passion to help empower others using fashion knowledge and expertise. This book is dedicated to my daughters, Elizabeth, Tatiana, and Chloe. You keep my heart singing! You are so filled with talent and ideas and it is such a thrill in my life to have your unending support. Love you more than you know!

Thank you also to my brilliant clients. It is my honor to serve you. I love reading your books, learning about your careers, meeting your families, and collaborating as co-creaters of new fashion design that works best for you!

ABOUT THE AUTHOR

Karen Mathis

Karen Mathis, Author, Fashion Stylist and Co-Owner of NSAI-Energy, loves being an entrepreneur. Her fashion merchandising career exposed her to large and smaller private corporate operations, including owning her own fashion businesses. Her personal mission is to use her fashion expertise to empower women.  She enjoys consulting, teaching, and writing as a way to share her experience and knowledge to help others. She works as a stylist and image consultant for a small private clientele. Karen lives in San Diego, CA with her husband, three daughters and three grandchildren.

Visit us: www.POWERofAppearance.com
Email us: Karen.PowerofAppearance@gmail.com
Like our Facebook Page:
https://www.facebook.com/PowerOfAppearance/
Tweet us: https://twitter.com/PowerAppearance
Listen to our Podcast: https://anchor.fm/powerofappearance
Check us out at LinkedIn:
https://www.linkedin.com/in/karenmathis/
Watch our Youtube Channel:
https://www.youtube.com/watch?v=6B-p8qi1Nus
Sign up for monthly wardrobe updates and fashion news:
https://powerofappearance.com/sign-up/

BOOKS BY THIS AUTHOR

Power Of Appearance

Did you know a first impression is made in a fraction of a second before eye contact or words are spoken? Being hired and being passed over for promotion can easily have roots in first impressions. Your appearance determines your first impression. Nonverbal communication plays such a role in how you are valued in the group, yet it's rarely discussed or taught. This book has two parts: The Story and The Science. It combines the psychology of how to dress for an audience and is supported by over 40 social psych studies. It solves the puzzle of how to dress your personal best with a step-by-step guide. Aesthetic rules derived from cultural experience are in play at all times whether aware or not. The reader learns along with the main character in The Story, how to apply both by using fashion stylist tools. Appearance power is like anything else when you know how to do it, it's easy!

8 Easy Pieces

Maximize your power and influence with how you dress. 8 EASY Pieces is a system that teaches women to become their own fashion stylist. Your new wardrobe will become your greatest asset. The book is organized with the greatest fashionista and the simplest fashion novice in mind. The first half of the book lays out filters for editing what you already own (what must stay and what must go), as well as developing what silhouettes look best on you. The second half includes real life examples like: packing for a trip, planning for a new job, or how the right eight pieces can

create 48 different outfits.

"Women are not to blame for clothing that does not work. Finding the key pieces that enhance your body shape, is an easy skill that is not taught." ~ Karen Mathis

Fashion Buyer

Do you want to know more about fashion merchandising from the inside? This E-book is loaded with timeless insight about the job of fashion buyer and the fashion industry. It has 102 vital questions answered in Q & A format covering everything from how to obtain your dream job (education, resume, the interview, etc.), to how to negotiate a vendor contract. "I opened the kimono to share both successes and failures," said Karen Mathis, author, and illustrator. Valuable resources and links are threaded throughout. Designer and famous quotes along with original art illustrations, enhance the reader's experience making this a fun way to learn more about fashion merchandising!

Darling, Where's Your Wrap?

This E-Book was created for inspiration and fashion fun. It includes over one hundred fashion art illustrations, many designer quotes, and wardrobe tips; on the subject of fashion scarves and wraps. The fashion illustrations, visually show new and renewed ways to wrap and tie scarves. Enjoy the artwork and the process of taking your wardrobe to the next level!

www.ingramcontent.com/pod-product-compliance
Lightning Source LLC
Chambersburg PA
CBHW040239220526
45473CB00001B/296